IMAGES
of England

BRIDGNORTH

High Street (Market Day). Bridgnorth

This is probably the most photographed scene in Bridgnorth, the High Street on market day when the street was still cobbled. The Town Hall can be seen in the background. Although the Town Hall has come to be the symbol of the town, it had humble beginnings as a barn in Much Wenlock, purchased to replace the original Town Hall destroyed in the siege during the Civil War, and rebuilt on new stone arches in the High Street in 1652.

The second most photographed structure in Bridgnorth is the bridge over the Severn. There has been a bridge on the site since the beginning of the twelfth century, but the present one dates from 1823, though it was widened in 1960. Before the bridge was built the river could be forded at Quatford.

IMAGES
of England

BRIDGNORTH

Compiled by
Alec Brew

TEMPUS

First published 2000
Copyright © Alec Brew, 2000

Tempus Publishing Limited
The Mill, Brimscombe Port,
Stroud, Gloucestershire, GL5 2QG

ISBN 0 7524 2075 5

Typesetting and origination by
Tempus Publishing Limited
Printed in Great Britain by
Midway Clark Printing, Wiltshire

Other books by Alec Brew in the Tempus Images of England series.

Albrighton and Shifnal
Wolverhampton, A Century of Change
Codsall and Claregate
Tettenhall and Pattingham
Penn and Blakenhall
Ettingshall and Monmore Green
Willenhall to Horseley Fields
Heath Town and Fallings Park
Bushbury and Featherstone
Staffordshire and Black Country Airfields
Shropshire Airfields (with Barry Abraham)

Contents

The Old Castle Inn on the western side of the High Street as it was in 1939. Most of this building was constructed immediately after the fire of 1646, and even incorporated some burnt timbers salvaged from the ruins of High Town. The Castle Inn and the Crown used to be the two principal inns of the town, and the Cheltenham to Liverpool coach used to call here twice daily.

A convenient stopping place on the road from Bridgnorth to Wolverhampton was the Wheel o' Worfield public house. The motor-bus service was started by the Great Western Railway and here a Milnes-Daimler bus stops for passengers on the way to Wolverhampton. These petrol driven buses started operating in April 1905, following six months of operation by three Clarkson steam-powered buses, which were not too successful.

Introduction

'Bridgnorth who shall fitly describe, seated, queen-like upon her rocky throne? In situation she has been likened to Old Jerusalem. Unique amongst English towns, unlike any other.' This was how the town was described by one Victorian visitor, and many such flowerey eulogies have been bestowed on Bridgnorth before and since.

One of the finest and most pleasing of English country towns, there are few which have so many buildings and places of interest concentrated in such a small area. Bridgnorth is in fact two towns, one above the other. High Town owes its allegiance to the high bluff which was a natural setting for the Norman castle which endured two major sieges, the first by the forces of the King just after its construction, and the second by forces opposed to the King during the Civil War.

Low Town clings to the banks of the River Severn, and the bridge which crosses it. This section of town therefore became an inland port, with warehouses and drinking dens for the bargemen who congregated there.

Either part of the town is interesting and well worth visiting in its own right, but the two taken together make Bridgnorth unique. They are linked by several flights of steps, the steep curving New Road, and the even steeper and winding Cartway. However the most interesting route is by taking the only inland Cliff Railway in Great Britain. When the Great Western Railway built their line from Kidderminster to Shrewsbury, passing underneath Bridgnorth, it put paid to the river traffic, but it brought something new – the tourists from the Black Country and elsewhere who began to flock to the country delights that were to be found within walking distance of Bridgnorth station. Now of course the railway is a major tourist attraction in its own right; reopened by enthusiasts as the Severn Valley Railway, it still carries tourists to the town from Kidderminster, but now tourists also come to the Bridgnorth just to see the railway.

The railway station is really in the village of Oldbury, which lay across a small valley from High Town, but is now just a suburb of its larger neighbour. Near the station is Panpudding Hill, an artificial mound on which the forces of King Henry I built a fort when they besieged Bridgnorth in 1102. The same hill was also a convenient place for the Roundheads to site their cannon during the Civil War siege.

Although usually thought of an a large country market town, Bridgnorth is actually also an engineering town of some standing. Sixty years before the Great Western Railway arrived, the castings for the first ever locomotive were made in the Mill Street Foundry for Richard Trevethick, and were completed twenty years before Stephenson's Rocket. There were other engineering companies like the nearby Eardington Iron Works, owing their location to the motive power provided by the river and the streams running into it.

One of the biggest industrial concerns in Bridgnorth was to become Southwell's Carpet Manufacturory, supplying carpets to Queen Victoria and winning gold medals for their designs. With the carpet factory now gone it is Star Aluminium, now Lawson Mardon Star, who have become the town's major industrial concern. Centred on an industrial estate on the Stourbridge Road, there is a matching industrial estate over the hill at Stanmore, on the site of the former RAF Bridgnorth. This Recruit Training Station was built as part of the Royal Air Force's major expansion just before the war and became the first taste of service life for squaddies for the next twenty years.

Bridgnorth residents often complain about the crowds of people who flock to the town on summer weekends from Wolverhampton and further afield, at least those who do not earn their living catering for the influx do so, but it is the price to be paid for living in one of the loveliest spots in England!

Alec Brew
2000

The Raven Hotel in Whitburn Street, 1938. One of the oldest inns in Bridgnorth, the Raven displays a tablet dated 1646.

One
High Town

High Town, Bridgnorth, owes its dominant location to Robert de Belleme, son of Roger de Montgomery, the Norman Earl who had been rewarded for his part in the invasion with the Lordship of Shropshire. Robert had been given a borough by his father, which was centred on Quatford. At this time Quatford was the local place to ford the river, and here Robert built a small motte-and-bailey castle. After his father's death Robert then built a splendid new castle at Bridgnorth, on a bluff overlooking the river.

The walled town of Bridgnorth grew to the north of the castle, and was known for obvious reasons as High Town, to differentiate it from other buildings which had been built by the river and bridge. The castle itself was demolished by the Parliamentarians after the Civil War siege, and much of High Town was destroyed by fire during the siege, so most of its buildings date from after this period. Luckily for Bridgnorth no further major development has been allowed to devastate the central heart of the town, and the seventeenth century streets of High Town retain their original charm.

A rare rear-view of the Town Hall at the turn of the nineteenth century with the Foster Memorial Institute, the three-gabled half-timbered building on the left. The Town Hall was used not only by the town council but also by the local assize. The Foster Institute was built in 1902 as a memorial to W.O. Foster of Apley Park, and contained reading and writing rooms, a billiard room, and ladies and mixed social rooms.

Bridgnorth railway station in the foreground with New Road behind rising up to the castle and St Mary's church. This view was taken in 1896 from Panpudding Hill showing the view the Parliamentarians had when they besieged the town during the Civil War.

North Gate sometime just after 1910, when the battlements were added during a refurbishment. North Gate was one of five entrances to the old walled town, and just before the Civil War the large room above was also used by the town council. The old fire station can be seen to the left, now a sports shop.

The slanting tower of Bridgnorth Castle as it appeared in 1896, with the church of St Mary Magdalene behind. The castle dates from 1101, when Robert de Belleme constructed it across the river from the castle that he had built at Quatford. The castle was destroyed by the Parliamentary forces after the surrender of Bridgnorth at the end of the Civil War siege, with the keep remaining at this perilous angle ever since.

A wider view of the castle keep and St Mary's church in 1896. The church was designed not by an architect but an engineer, Thomas Telford, which is perhaps why it looks so unusual with a dome set upon a square tower supported by columns.

Bridgnorth Infirmary at the beginning of the nineteenth century. It had been opened in 1896, superseding an older building in Listley Street.

An advertisement for Arthur Jones' Castle Restaurant at the turn of the twentieth century, when it had been in business for thirty-four years. It was on the corner of Postern Gate and East Castle Street, and later became Whitfield's electrical shop, but has now reverted to becoming the Castle tea-rooms. As shown in this advertisement Arthur Jones operated a second restaurant at the time at No. 12 High Street, near North Gate.

Bridgnorth Post Office around 1905. It opened in 1901, and the White Lion Inn can be seen next door.

The bell-ringers at St Leonard's church in 1912, having won the Glasbury Bell-ringing Competition.

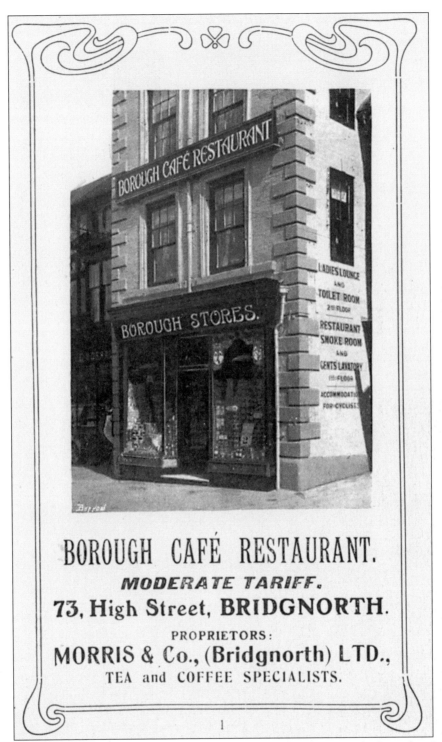

An advertisement for the Borough Cafe Restaurant in the High Street. It had a Ladies' Lounge and 'Toilet Room' on the second floor with a 'Gents Lavatory' on the first floor. The building, which sticks out slightly from its neighbours, is now occupied by Sketchleys.

The teachers at Bridgnorth Grammar School in 1913. From left to right, back row: Mr 'Crossie' Crossland, Basil Simmonds (art), Mr E.T. 'Slasher' Smith (geography), -?-. Front row: Basil Jakeman (chemistry), Revd H.V. Dawes (headmaster), Mr Wake (french and german). The Revd Dawes lived at Severn Brow, Oldbury, where twenty boarders were lodged, and E.T. Smith kept the boarding house at St Leonard's Close.

One class at Bridgnorth Grammar School in 1913. Unfortunately the name of the teacher is unknown and is believed to have been at the school for only a short time before going off to war.

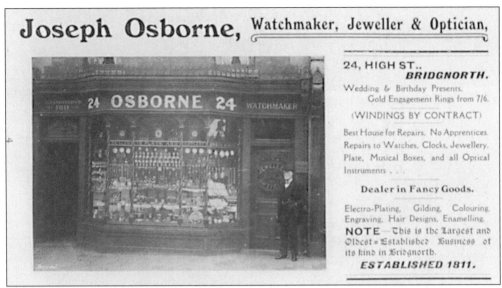

Joseph Osborne, Watchmaker, Jeweller & Optician,

24, HIGH ST.,
BRIDGNORTH.

Wedding & Birthday Presents.
   Gold Engagement Rings from 7/6.

(WINDINGS BY CONTRACT)

Best House for Repairs. No Apprentices.
Repairs to Watches, Clocks, Jewellery,
Plate, Musical Boxes, and all Optical
Instruments . . .

Dealer in Fancy Goods.

Electro-Plating. Gilding. Colouring.
Engraving. Hair Designs. Enamelling.
NOTE—This is the Largest and
Oldest-Established Business of
its kind in Bridgnorth.
ESTABLISHED 1811.

Joseph Osborne's shop in the High Street in 1900, in business as a watchmaker, jeweller and optician since 1811. This building, No. 24 High Street, is now occupied by Dewhurst's the butchers, with a new shopfront featuring a single large window.

The grounds of Bridgnorth Castle before the First World War, formerly of course the site of the original castle. The land was established as a town park with a bandstand as a gift to the town by W.O. Foster in 1897. It was opened as part of the celebrations of Queen Victoria's Diamond Jubilee. In 1956 they were extended on the occasion of the 800th anniversary of the foundation of the borough.

St Leonards School Infants III class around 1929. In the middle row fourth left is George Fewtrell, and fifth left is his half sister, Irene Mary Hatton. Second from the left on the front row is Arthur Lowe, (but not Capt. Mainwaring from *Dad's Army!*).

Budgen Hall, photographed from its courtyard in 1937. The Hall was built in 1730 on the southern side of Listley Street by William Budgen a local merchant. The garden ran down the hillside, and William Budgen planed a vineyard there, the eastern part of which was only removed when the railway tunnel was constructed in 1865.

The choir and clergy at St Leonard's church in 1932.

The view along the High Street towards North Gate during the 1920s with garages on both sides of the road.

The site of Whitburn Gate, one of the six original gates in the Town Wall (at the end of Whitburn Street) as it was in 1937. Part of the stonework of the gate can be seen beneath the brickwork of the house in the foreground. The steps of the houses further along needed to be built when the gate was removed in 1761, because the road surface was then lowered.

Deighton & Smith

Pharmaceutical and Family Chemists,

BRIDGNORTH.

The Dispensing Establishment.

35, HIGH STREET, BRIDGNORTH.

Telegraphic Address:— DEIGHTON SMITH, BRIDGNORTH.

3

Deighton & Smith's Pharmaceutical Chemists at No. 35 High Street, at the turn of the century. This building was later occupied by Boots the Chemist until they moved alongside the Town Hall. It is now occupied by the Edinburgh Woollen Mill.

A class of children at St Leonard's School photographed for the Coronation of King George VI in 1937.

The Sixth Form at Bridgnorth Grammar School just after the Second World War, with Mr Jakeman, the headmaster, in the centre. The Grammar School is now the Endowed School.

A picture of the Town Hall and High Street on market day (see p. 9 for an earlier photograph of the same scene). Now in the 1950s vans have brought the produce into town, rather than by carts. Boots the Chemist faces the Swan Hotel.

A Daimler diesel bus on the route from Wolverhampton after attempting to pass beneath the Town Hall on 16 May 1949. The High Street has recently been made a one way street, and so traffic is no longer able to pass under the Town Hall. The route has now been blocked off with bollards.

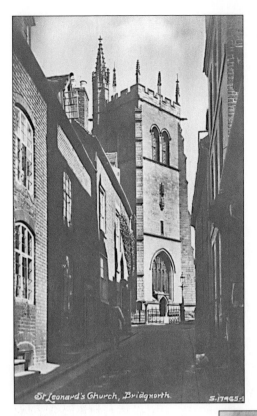

St Leonard's Church, Bridgnorth. S.17965-1

A photograph of St Leonard's church taken from Church Street. There has been a church on the site from the twelfth century, but the original church was badly damaged during the Civil War siege. The present building dates from the reconstruction of the original church in the nineteenth century. The red sandstone quarried nearby is a marked contrast to the stone used in St Mary's at the other end of High Town.

Mr Samuel Brighton, aged seventy-five, a well-known market trader with an antique stall. Pictured in 1957 Mr Brighton had been running his stall at Bridgnorth market for thirty years, even though he was based at Castlefields, Shrewsbury.

The staff of Nock Deighton and Sons, the auctioneers, gathered outside their premises in 1953, suitably decorated for the Coronation of Queen Elizabeth. Inset is a Coronation medal.

The interior of St Mary Magdalene's church in 1955, much more light and airy than St Leonards, with large clear glass windows on each side, affording fine views across the river valley to the east.

The view along East Castle Street to St Mary Magdalene's church in the 1950s. Looking the other way the tower of St Leonard's can be seen across the rooftops of the High Street.

The site of Listley Gate, the smallest of the six gates in the Town Wall, at the top of what is now Railway Street. It was demolished after the siege of 1646.

The girls of the Infants II Class at St Leonard's School during the 1950s.

The opening of the new fat pig livestock market on 24 August 1952, by the Mayor, Alderman J.W.C. Bowers, with Capt Milner Deighton in attendance. The livestock market has always been an important strand of the town's livelihood.

The ninety-six children of Star Aluminium's Container Department workers at their annual party at St Leonard's Hall on 27 January 1979.

The visit of Ray Reardon, six-times World Snooker Champion, to the Old Comrades Club in Listley Street. From left to right: Jim Mitchell, Eric Brown, George Downes, Roger Dickin, Chris Lewis, Jock Patterson, Mike Rogers, Jim Cannaby, Ray Reardon, Dave Winwood, Chris Jephson, Jim Rogers.

The choir and clergy for the last service at St Leonard's church in 1976. The town could no longer support two large Anglican churches so St Leonard's closed. It is now kept open by the Redundant Churches Conservation Trust, a voluntary organization which welcomes visitors, not to mention donations!

Two

Low Town

Low Town owes its existence to the River Severn and the bridge which was built across it. The first bridge was built in the early part of the twelfth century, and the current one in 1823. In the days when rivers provided the only means of bulk transport, sites like Bridgnorth became important inland ports, with warehouses to gather in the industrial and agricultural produce of the area.

The river at Bridgnorth is often so shallow that barges were stuck there for weeks at a time, and the many inns and hostelries took good advantage of this and profited by entertaining the bargeman. Only a small part of Low Town is gathered on the western side of the river nestling under the cliff, and in times past there were cave dwellings actually cut into the soft sandstone. Most of Low Town is on the other bank, and had expanded rapidly during the latter half of the nineteenth century, spreading slowly up the valley side nearly to the Hermitage.

A view across the bridge as it was before the First World War, towards the Cliff Railway in the centre, and High Town looming over Underhill Street. The 'Ridley's Seeds' building then featured a number of different advertisements, including Salt & Co.'s Burton Ales, and Morral's Whiskey. Facing the bridge is McMichael & Barker's grocers shop, next to the Vaults public house.

A view looking down the Hermitage Hill towards Low Town taken around 1896 when there were far fewer trees on the lower slopes. The traveller from Wolverhampton is afforded this fine view as he drops into the valley. The two churches, St Mary's on the left and St Leonard's on the right, face each other across the roofs of High Town.

THE HERMITAGE (Custodian's Cottage). (See page 30). *A. W. W. Ball, Photo.*

The Custodian's cottage at the Hermitage, around the turn of the twentieth century. Although living in a cave, like many in Bridgnorth at the time, the Custodian and his family enjoyed the fine view of Bridgnorth as seen in the previous picture. They would have been blessed with glorious sunsets beyond the town, with the Shropshire countryside stretching away to the Clee Hills and the distant blue mountains of Wales.

A view from St Leonard's across the gasworks, built on the site of a boatyard next to the river to enable the delivery of coal by barge. In the background beneath High Rock is the water pumping station, which pumped water from a well into a reservoir. To the left is Fort Pendlestone, William Whitmore's mill, built in the 1850s to look like a castle.

Bridgnorth. *Stoneway Steps*   Valentines Series   21 320

The most photographed of the three series of steps joining Low Town with High Town are the Stoneway Steps, which cut through the solid rock in places, and are here buttressed with the iron 'Pope's Spectacles', cast in Bridgnorth Foundry. Though taken before the First World War, this picture is timeless!

The easy way between Low Town and High Town, is the Cliff Railway, opened on 7 July 1892, the only inland such railway in Great Britain. The route was cut through the solid sandstone, and nearby houses had to have their walls reinforced. It was originally water powered; a water tank on the roof of each carriage was filled at the top station from a 30,0000 gallon reservoir, sufficient for its weight to haul up the lower carriage. At the bottom the water was emptied out, to be pumped back up to the top station.

Castle Hill Railway, Bridgnorth

Alongside the original road between High Town and Low Town, the Cartway, is 'Bishop Percy's house, a timber-framed building constructed in 1580, and the birthplace of Thomas Percy who later became Bishop of Dromore in Ireland. It was the only major building west of the river to survive the fire of 1646. It is shown here at the beginning of the nineteenth century when it was being used as Charles Rushton's Iron Foundry. More recently it became Bridgnorth Boy's Club.

Colonel Thorneycroft of Tettenhall Towers was a rich industrialist whose family had made their money in iron and steel. In the late nineteenth century he erected a wooden bungalow on Bylet Island in the Severn, which he called the Sabrina Bungalow after the spirit of the river, He used it as a base for his boat which he kept on the river. It later became the clubhouse for the Bylet Bowling Club.

The Bylet Bowling Club was formed in 1885 after the then tenant of Bylet Island, W. Roberts, had obtained permission to turn the island into a recreation centre, then reached by a small ferry boat from the east side of the bridge. These are the members of the Bylet Bowling Club in 1890.

St Mary's School was originally situated at the end of Severn Street. These are the boys and girls of Group II around 1929.

St Mary's Group III poses for their picture in 1932.

The view from Castle Walk over Low Town in the 1930s. The bowling green on Bylet Island can be seen to the lower right. In the centre are the seed warehouses which are now the Old Mill Antique Centre, and in the top left is High Rock.

A pre-First World War advertisement for H.S. Pass, a coal, lime and salt merchant of Underhill Street, who brought his coal from Cannock Chase, probably by canal and river, and then delivered it by cart.

A Guy SD motor bus, No. 73, passing up Hermitage Hill in 1928. Wolverhampton Corporation Transport Department had taken over the route from GWR in 1923, using Tilling-Stevens vehicles initially. Four Wolverhampton-built Guys were introduced on the route from 1925.

A Class Group at St Mary's School gathered to celebrate the Coronation of King George VI in 1937.

A gathering of local mayors at the Bylet Bowling Club in 1948. From left to right, standing: Col. S.J. Thompson, Lt-Gen. Sir Oliver Leese, Mr T.C. Pembro (the Bridgnorth Town Crier). Seated: the Mayors of Bilston, Bridgnorth and Much Wenlock, together with their wives.

The Lift & Severn Bridge, Bridgnorth

The Cliff Railway viewed from the upper end, after its operation and conversion to electric winding in 1944, but before the new streamlined carriages were introduced in 1955.

An aerial view of the Pale Meadow Printing Works (centre) which had been taken over by Radio Gramophone Developments (RGD) during the war to make radar and other secret electrical gear. After the war it became AT & E, then Racal, and by the time this picture was take, Decca. Note the circle of children on the playground of St Mary's School in the foreground.

One of the major employers in the town from 1828 was the Carpet Manufacturing Company, or H. & M. Southwell. Here members of staff gather for a photograph in Coronation Year, 1953.

The retirement presentation to Mr E.G. Head, Departmental Manager at Southwell's Carpet factory in 1959. Note the gasworks alongside, which had been nationalized in 1949.

Revellers at the Bridgnorth & District Young Farmer's Club Dance in 1957. The venue is not known, but many of the people in this picture came from the Quatford area.

In 1954 Star Aluminium purchased sixty acres of land alongside the Old Worcester Road to build a new rolling mill, which came into operation in 1956. Star had been formed in 1933 on the site of the old Star Engineering Factory in Wolverhampton, which produced Star cars and gave its name to the new factory, producing principally aluminium foil. This aerial view shows the factory in 1962, when it had already expanded considerably, becoming the major industrial concern in the town.

A gathering for an official civic visit to Star Aluminium in 1962, including the Mayor and Mayoress of Bridgnorth, councillors, town officials, representatives of suppliers, the Press, and company officials. After a tour of the factory the visitors were entertained to lunch in a local hotel.

The view is taken from High Town over the bridge around 1950, well before most of the development had taken place in Low Town.

A Star Rugby team playing the Bridgnorth Rugby Club in their annual fixture, in 1969. Despite their inexperience, Star were leading at half-time and were only narrowly defeated.

A charity football match between Star Aluminium and the Gaylords All Stars which including ex-Wolves and England players Jimmy Mullen and Eddie Clamp; held at Codsall Village Hall ground, December 1969. The match was in aid of Joe Thomas who had been badly injured keeping goal for Star. The Star only lost 3-2, with Jimmy Mullen scoring the winner.

The old route from Low Town to High Town as it looked in 1937. This was the site of the West Gate, otherwise known as St Mary's Gate or Hungary Gate. It is at the junctions of Listley Street, St Mary's Street and Pound Street but the gatehouse was demolished in 1821. It is now the site of a mini-roundabout. The other main routes between the towns were up the Cartway to Cow Gate, and through the small Listley Gate.

Some of the contributors to Star Aluminium's company magazine, 1969.

The retirement party for Mr T.W. Head, H. & M. Southwell's managing director, held at the Friars, Bridgnorth in 1929.

St Mary's Steps climb past a number of picturesque cottages, the occupants of which pay for their fine views across the valley by having to climb or descend the many steps whenever they leave their door, the only inhabitants of Bridgnorth for which the Cliff Railway is of little help!

The fields between Low Town and High Rock have in recent times become Severn Park recreation ground and the home of Bridgnorth Rugby Club.

The machine shop of AT & E in the Pale Meadow Works in the 1950s. From left to right: Fred Underhill, Eddie Elcock, Bruce Gibbons, John Constable.

The retired employees of Star Aluminium (nowadays Lawson Mardon Star) gathered for their annual dinner in 1980.

Apley Park around 1902, an exotic early nineteenth-century Gothic mansion, built as an extension to a Georgian manor house at Stockton, upstream of Bridgnorth. It was once considered as a home for Queen Adelaide after the death of her husband William IV, but it was decided that the fogs from the river would affect her health.

The Container Division of Star Aluminium's float in the 1980 Bridgnorth Carnival. This one depicts *Dr Who* characters, which won first prize in the trade section. Dr Who is second on the left, and the 'spaceman' next to him is Roger Franklin. His suit was a pair of overalls sprayed with aluminium paint, but it split around the middle when he was climbing into it, and needed a quick repair job with sellotape!

Decca's Pale Meadow Works in the 1980s shortly after its closure. It was sold to the Taiwanese company Tatung, who immediately decamped to the rate-free environment of the Telford Enterprise Zone.

Decca's chimney, not imitating the angle of the castle keep, but on its way down, as the site is cleared for housing.

Three
The River Severn

Being the longest river in England at 220 miles long, the River Severn has been a major transport route since Bronze age times. For most of that time it has provided a convenient route for the flat-bottomed sailing barges which could ply upriver as far as Wales, and down to the sea. Most of the towns along its route have prospered because of this, including Bridgnorth.

But a river is also a barrier, and this means riverside towns blessed with a bridge have a double importance, being intersected by both land and water routes. The first bridge in the area was probably at Quatford just downstream, but even before the building of a bridge, this would have been the best local place to ford the river. Bridgnorth probably got its name because its bridge was north of that at Quatford, which has now lost its bridge completely. The first bridge downstream these days is now the footbridge at Arley.

The river was also an important source of food, and the best way to catch fish in reasonable quantities was in traps. A relic of the era when the Severn had fish traps at various places along its length still survives at Bridgnorth. To enable boats to pass the traps, canals were built around them to let boats by, and Bylet Island is the result of the construction of one of these. It is only in more recent times that rivers have been seen as places of recreation, for fishing and boating, even in times past swimming; though now in more safety conscious days, swimming is severely discouraged in the Severn's dangerous swirling eddies.

An engraving of Bridgnorth done in 1824 with most of the familiar elements, the slanting castle keep, the two churches, the bridge, and a local fisherman. The shallowness of the river at Bridgnorth often caused barges to congregate there for days or even weeks as they waited for the river level to rise, and the riverside pubs earned reputations as bad as any dockside drinking dens.

The bridge with its ornamental iron railings on the central arches. In the foreground is the old quay, the dock which made Bridgnorth an inland port. The building at the far end of the bridge, opposite the clock tower is advertising 'Mazanattee Tea'. The last barge on the river, carrying firebricks from Ironbridge, hit the bridge in 1895 when the helmsman was distracted, and sank, lying rotting for many years just below the bridge.

Darley's Landing place, opposite the Carpet Factory. The company hired out rowing boats, and also operated pleasure boats along the river.

The Severn where it curves below the hill known as High Rock. At the foot of the hill is the water-pumping station, which takes the town's water not from the river but from a well. The fields to the right are now the Severn Park.

High Town as seen from the far end of the bridge in the 1920s, with the houses disposed along St Mary's Steps rising up the hill, and the Castle Walk running along the top.

Col. Thomas Thorneycroft (right) inspecting Bylet Island before the construction of his bungalow. The Bylet was an artifically created island, made by constructing a canal on the east side, along which river boats could pass avoiding the wickerwork fish traps sited across the main stream. It dates from medieval times.

The Sabrina Bungalow erected by Col. Thorneycroft on the western side of Bylet Island in 1901.

All along this section of the Severn there are houses cut into the soft sandstone of each bank, often with brickwork front rooms. The Hermitage was an early one, but there were many more in Bridgnorth itself. Rock Cottage was sited opposite Apley Park upstream of the town, and was still occupied when photographed here in the 1920s. None of these 'cave dwellings' are now inhabited.

Bridgnorth viewed from Knowle Sands to the south, at the turn of the twentieth century.

Although it seems incredible now, bathing in the river was encouraged in the 1920s to the extent that a diving board was sited next to the eastern end of the bridge. Most of these happy swimmers had travelled out from Wolverhampton but one of the men in the water was a local man, Len Seaward. The vicious eddies in the river which have taken many lives, mean swimming is now strictly discouraged.

This is Walter Cooper aged seventy-four, who kept the café at Quatford, and was a well-known fisherman on the Severn for forty-five years. He is pictured after catching a $13\frac{1}{2}$lb pike which had infested his favourite roach pool for a long time. He armed himself with a pike rod and bait, and managed to catch it after several weeks, but it broke his tackle! He caught it at the second attempt.

Flooding is a regular trial for those who live near the river at Bridgnorth. Here, in the 1950s, the waters are washing over Underhill Street, and will have covered the Bylet Island just below the bridge, putting paid to the bowling for a while!

This is not a road repair gang during a period of such flooding, but the Sir Alfred MacAlpine entrant in the annual Ironbridge to Bridgnorth raft race. They are being pulled in to the side at Severn Park, after a trying time through Jackfield rapids. Members of the crew include Peter Brew, Rob Mottram, Roger Nicholls, John Lee, Trevor Smart, John Whitham, Ray Willetts and Ron Carter.

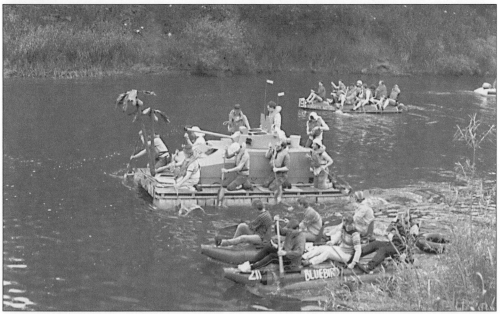

Here three contestants in the 1985 race are neck and neck with *GKN-Sankey*, just leading Verdotti Motors and *Bluebird*. *GKN-Sankey* sank – not surprisingly as they were carrying two palm trees and a tank!

Four
Oldbury

Facing the castle on the other side of a small valley is the village of Oldbury, mainly astride the Cleobury Mortimor Road. With its own small church it was a quiet rural community occasionally beset by armies besieging the adjacent town. It inherited an artificial hill shaped like an upturned pudding bowl, and called not surprisingly Panpudding Hill. When the railway came however, Bridgnorth Station was built on the Oldbury side of the little valley, and was eventually joined to Castle Hill by a footbridge. As the focus of the town began to shift away from the river and towards the railway, the importance of little Oldbury grew. New housing estates, built in more recent years, have firmly adhered the village to the rest of Bridgnorth, so that it is more a suburb than the first small village on the road to Cleobury Mortimer.

Bridgnorth railway station as it appeared in 1915, with the iron footbridge crossing the valley to the New Road and the castle keep and St Mark Magdalene's church on Castle Hill. New Road was first cut in 1786, and widened in 1876, with the footbridge being built to connect with it in 1896.

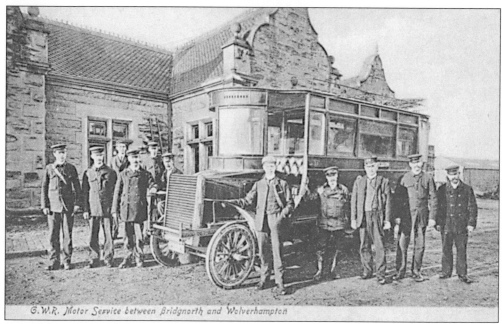

G.W.R. *Motor Service between Bridgnorth and Wolverhampton*

One of the GWR's Clarkson steam-powered buses outside Bridgnorth railway station sometime between 7 November 1904 and April 1905. GWR bus and rail staff are gathered around it. These buses had great difficulty getting up the Hermitage, and were soon withdrawn from the route to Wolverhampton.

This photograph was taken in the same location as the one above, and also shows the same gathering of bus and rail staff, but this bus is a double-decker Daimler operated by Wolverhampton Corporation, who took over the Bridgnorth route in 1923. The photograph was taken during the Second World War, by which time RAF Bridgnorth had been built, and these buses carried a high proportion of the squaddies under training.

Eversley House on the Cleobury Mortimer Road in Oldbury. During the 1940s, 50s and 60s this was the home of J.D. North, one of the great pioneers of British aviation. He was chief designer at the Grahame White Co. in 1913, later moving to Boulton & Paul of Norwich. When the aircraft department was sold off he became managing director of the resulting Boulton Paul Aircraft, which moved to Wolverhampton in 1936. By the time of his death in 1968, he had become chairman of the company. One of his great passions was rock gardens, and he had a fine one at Eversley House.

Eardington FC Captain, Ernie Bourne, receiving the H.E. Whitney Cup from Geoff Whitney in the 1957-1958 season. Eardington lies just south of Oldbury, the site of a well-known iron works in the days when charcoal was used to fire the blast furnaces.

Four locomotives (LMS 2-6-0, 46443, GWR 0-6-0, 3205, LMS 2-6-0, 43106, and LMS 2-8-0, 8233,) await the re-opening of the Severn Valley Railway in 1969. Closed by Dr Beeching, the southern half of the Kidderminster to Shrewsbury line was re-opened as the Severn Valley Railway by enthusiasts, and remains a major tourist attraction in the Severn valley.

Work under way in the workshops of the Severn Valley Railway in Bridgnorth, as old steam engines are brought back to life, and maintained to professional standards.

Work under way on the new bridge over the Severn which would carry the Bridgnorth by-pass over the river from the autumn of 1984. The bridge is 270m long, with a main span of 66m over the river, and was built by the Wolverhampton company, Sir Alfred MacAlpine.

The railway also needed a new bridge to accommodate the by-pass, and here *Raveningham Hall* crosses the new bridge with work on the by-pass going on below.

The same engine, the 4-6-0 modified Hall class *Raveningham Hall*, approaching Foley Park Tunnel as it nears Kidderminster in the winter of 1990.

The footbridge to the railway station was condemned as unsafe and dismantled in 1976. A small section serves as an ornament on the roundabout at the start of the Bridgnorth by-pass. This new bridge was built to replace it, and here Joey Brew poses with the station behind him in the winter of 1998.

Five

Quatford

In Saxon times Quatford was considered a more important place than Bridgnorth. A community was established here as it was considered the best local place to ford the River Severn. It was also the base for Roger de Belleme when his father created a borough for him just after the Norman Invasion. Roger built a motte and bailey castle there, which he abandoned after inheriting his father's estates, in favour of a new stone castle just upstream at Bridgnorth.

Quatford still has a castle, but it is a mock castle built in 1830 by John Smalman. The castle, like much of the pleasant village of Quatford, is lost to view behind the wooded hills on the eastern side of the Severn valley. The old winding main road was replaced in the 1960s by a new road, and this helped even more to hide Quatford church and other village buildings from passing motorists. The people of Quatford like it that way of course, quite happy that their larger neighbour, Bridgnorth, has taken over their former pre-eminence in the local part of the Severn Valley.

Cottages on the main Kidderminster Road at Quatford, c. 1920.

Quatford House, a Georgian country house set back from the main road. Behind the house is a walled kitchen garden with a row of greenhouses along one side. From these entry can be gained to the Quatford 'leper caves', a complex series of rooms cut into the sandstone cliff, with a deep underground well, and sandstone 'bunks' cut into the walls. These are actually a folly, built by Mr Smalman of Quatford Castle.

The children and teachers of Quatford Church Sunday School, July 1944.

The old Quatford schoolhouse, which was demolished in 1960 to make way for the new Kidderminster Road through the village.

A photograph of the old Quatford Vicarage also demolished for building of the new road. The old road was narrow and winding and cut through solid sandstone in places, as can be seen here, where it passed the churchyard on the left.

The original Severn Valley Café at Quatford, which began in 1948 as a tea stall started by Walter Cooper and his daughter Mrs Smallman. This original wooden building was replaced with a brick structure in 1963.

Some of the guests at the opening of the new Severn Valley Café on 10 June 1963. The café is now rented to Trust House Forte, and is operated as a Little Chef.

The interior of the old Severn Valley Café, before demolition, and ready for lunch in 1962 with Rose Clee and Gill Price eager to serve.

Quatford Village in 1960 showing the new road to the left and the old road to the right.

An aerial view of the Severn Valley Café (central) with caravan parks on either side of the main road, stretching down to the River Severn.

An aerial view of 'Roccabrun' which means 'The house by the Red Cliff' – for obvious reasons.

The old oak tree on Hill House Farm, a remnant of the old Morfe Forest, and supposedly the place where the Norman Earl Roger de Montgomery met his wife Adeliza. Travelling from Normandy she had been beset by a severe storm in the Channel, and had vowed that if she survived she would found a church at the place where she met her betrothed. They met under a tree in Quatford and she founded St Mary Magdalene's church, though obviously a little way away from the oak!

An aerial view of Quatford House to the left and Quatford Castle to the right. Though not a 'proper castle', having been built by John Smalman in 1830, its mock battlements echo the first castle built in the area by Roger de Belleme – a motte and bailey construction – used to guard the local ford in the river. However this was not the earliest known settlement as the Danes camped here even earlier in the winter of 896-897.

Dr Barbara Moore marching into Quatford in January 1960, on her famous John O'Groats to Lands End Walk. She stopped at St Mary's School in Low Town to ask a policeman the location of the nearest telephone box, and was directed to the one in Quatford, which was on her route. There she made a call to her husband, though local villagers were gathered all around. The whole walk was completed in three weeks.

The Danery Inn public house, Quatford, as it was in 1979. It is a 300-year-old inn, now lying on a lay-by of the new road, formed from a curve of the old. In 1971 it had been run for the Wilkinsons for twenty-eight years, and before that by the Poole family (Mrs Wilkinson's relatives) for the previous seventy-five years.

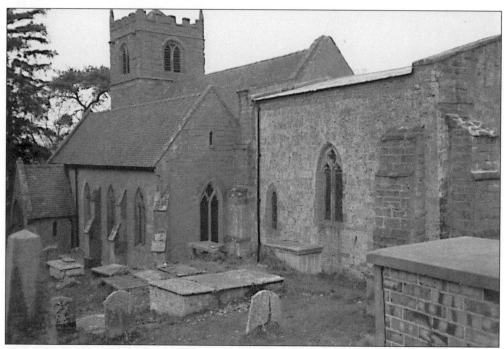

The rear of St Mary Magdalene's church in Quatford. The original church can clearly be seen even though it was built 900 years ago, before the forward extension was added.

The thirty-three steps which lead up to the entrance to Quatford church. Just to the left of these can be seen a well cut in the solid rock, the top of which is 6ft above the road level, which has been cut through the rock alongside.

Six
Stanmore

Before 1939 Stanmore was just an area of agricultural land to the east of the Severn Valley, inheriting its name from Stanmore Hall. Then the Royal Air Force arrived, and built a camp for the initial training of new recruits as part of the large expansion scheme. As there was already an RAF Stanmore in Middlesex, the station was given the name RAF Bridgnorth.

There never was an airfield at RAF Bridgnorth, though Alan Cobham had brought his flying circus to a field near the Old Worcester Road, not far away, in 1935. However later on, especially in the post-war years, there were usually aircraft to be found at Stanmore; 'gate guardians' and others dotted about the camp, no doubt to inspire the recruits.

Though only built as a temporary camp, largely of wooden huts, RAF Bridgnorth survived after the war with more permanent buildings and hangars appearing. It was the first taste of RAF life for many a new recruit; and therefore firmly etched onto their memories. It closed in 1963, after the end of National Service and the general run-down of the Royal Air Force. An industrial estate and a country park now occupy the site.

Nowadays the main claim to fame for Stanmore is the fine Motor Museum, established in 1976 at Stanmore Hall, open every weekend.

The main gates to RAF Bridgnorth after the entrance had been considerably improved during the 1950s. Guarding the gate to the left can be seen Hawker Hurricane IIc, LF686, one of a number of aircraft dotted round the camp over the years. This aircraft was later sent to the Smithsonian Air and Space Museum in Washington DC in exchange for a Hawker Typhoon.

The main guard room also in the 1950s, the inside of which most squaddies hoped to avoid. Like most buildings in the camp it was a 'temporary' wooden hut.

A passing out parade during the 1950s. There were two parade grounds in the camp. In the far upper corner of the ground there is a Spitfire.

The granting of the Freedom of the Town of Bridgnorth to RAF Bridgnorth on 12 April 1950. The ceremony is taking place in front of the Crown Hotel in the High Street, and the Mayor, Councillor M.A. Banks, is presenting the scroll conferring the Freedom of Entry to the Station Commander Group Captain G.J.L. Read. The presentation was the highlight of a week of celebrations.

A common photograph, one of the squaddies standing in front of one of the aircraft dotted around the camp, in this case a Hawker Hurricane, though a different one from that at the main gate.

The main entrance to RAF Bridgnorth in earlier times, before the brick pillars and iron gates were erected. The road into the camp is flanked by two 'gate guardians', a Hurricane and a de Havilland Vampire jet fighter.

Before the coming of the Royal Air Force, the area round Stanmore was entirely agricultural in nature. This is reaping and binding on one of the local farms in the 1920s.

In the 1920s grass track motor bike racing was very popular in the area, and this is a rider approaching the finish line at a meeting at Rushmere. What is not clear is whether he is doing tricks or whether he is inadvertently parting company with his bike!

Stanmore Hall as it appeared around 1978 at the time when partners Bob Roberts and Mike Barker were setting up their Midland Motor Museum there. They had owned a number of vintage racing cars for some time, racing them at vintage meetings and the museum therefore was a logical extension of their interest.

The 1933 Napier-Railton 24 litre which holds the all-time lap record for Brooklands at 143.44mph, though capable of an outright 180mph. This was one of the early exhibits in the museum, and is shown in the purpose-built exhibition hall. It was later sold in Germany, and was bought back by another owner for £1 million!

Seven

Highley

Highley and the villages around it were set on a small coalfield, and there was mining in the area as far back as the eighteenth century. It was the coming of the GWR's Severn Valley railway line, opened in 1862, which really started something of a boom in the area. Now that coal could be easily transported to all parts of the country, new mining companies were set up, and miners flocked to the area from the Black Country, the Potteries and Scotland. The local quiet, rural villages were expanded into coal mining communities of which Highley was the largest and most important. By 1921 there were about 2,000 people living in the village, but from then the mining industry began a decline which lead to the closure of the Highley mine in 1940, and the last pit in the area, across the river at Alveley in 1969.

Highley and its neighbouring villages have changed once again, partly back to villages serving the local agricultural economy, but more importantly to dormitory communities for Bridgnorth and larger towns further afield.

The Ship Hotel at Stanley, an almost separate village to Highley, on the banks of the Severn. The photograph has been taken from across the river at Alveley, which is connected to the west bank by a ferry. The Ship's name reflects its use by bargemen, though in the eighteenth century it was called the Royal George.

One of the original sixteen stone cottages at the hamlet of New England, though eight had been knocked down by the turn of the century. They had been built around 1800 for the workers at Billingsley Colliery, but by 1909 when these photographs were taken, the remaining eight were mostly used by farmworkers. This is believed to be the Walford family, with Nancy Walford holding her grandson Eric. There was a washhouse at each end of the terrace.

Another of the cottages housed another member of the Walford family, who is posing here with what is possibly his housekeeper. Though the houses were all in one terrace they were not identical as can be seen from the differing windows.

This is the Burgess family in another of the cottages, which were all knocked down in 1917, because the sewage works was built nearby. The terrace lay on the lane to the ford in Borle Brook with their gardens over the road. Note the moleskin trousers hanging over the rail.

The New Inns Hotel in Highley High Street, sometime before 1905. This inn opened in 1839, hoping to gain from the fact that the Ship Hotel was not centrally located. The Bache family kept it for seventy-five years, and is now renamed in their honour the Bache Arms.

Colliers beneath the headgear of Billingsley Colliery, which was first recorded in 1797. The colliery got a rail link to the Severn Valley line in 1903 and kept working until 1922.

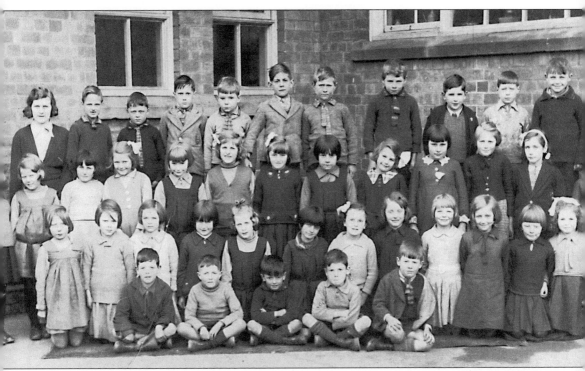

The pupils of one class of Highley Council School in the 1930s, with the class teacher, Mildred Walford, on the left of the back row. The school had been greatly expanded in 1897 to take 270 pupils.

The Waterfall, Borle Brook, Highley

The waterfall which used to exist on the Borle Brook which ran down to the Severn, downstream of Stanley.

The beautiful fourteenth-century St Peter's church at Chelmarsh, north of Highley. This photograph was taken around 1900 but the scene looks absolutely identical today; even the gravestones lean at the same angle.

Church Road Highley in the 1930s. These houses were part of the expansion of the village caused by the opening of the coalmine in 1879.

Woodhill Road in the Garden Village, Highley. Built on Woodhill Farm, the Garden Village was a venture of the Billingsly Colliery Company, but unfortunately was not finished when the company was liquidated just after the First World War.

St John the Baptist church at Kinlet around the year 1900. Beautifully situated near Kinlet Hall (now Moffat's School), the church looks very much the same today, although the railings round the grave of Sarah Green of Hammond Hall are no longer there, and the churchyard cross was restored in 1921 as a memorial to those locals who died in the First World War.

The Eagle and Serpent public house in Kinlet. Though this looks for all the world like a photograph dating from the 1950s, it is in fact modern, the vintage cars being owned by the publican. Only the style of the pub name gives the game away.

An aerial view of part of the garden village in Highley taken around 1960. By then the Highley pit had been closed for twenty years, but many Highley men still crossed the river to work at the Alveley Pit, until that too closed in 1969.

The darts team at the Miner's Arms in Bagginswood, winners of the Cleobury Mortimer and District Darts League in 1953.

The naming of an engine in honour of British Military Railwaymen, on Highley station.

Highley station as it appeared in 1990. Fully restored by the Severn Valley Railway, the station lies nearer the riverside hamlet of Stanley than Highley. It was the coming of the railway which brought the real coal mining boom to the area.

Eight

Arley

Unlike the other communities covered by this book, Arley is not in Shropshire, but just over the border in Worcestershire. However it has been included in this collection because Arley station on the Severn Valley railway line, the line which links all the communities along the river valley, is the last one on the western side of the river (or the first one depending on whether it is an 'up' train or a 'down' train you are sitting on!).

Bridgnorth might be described as the 'capital' of this section of the Severn valley, and though most of Arley village is on the other side of the river, the station side looks to Bridgnorth rather than the Worcestershire towns of Bewdley and Kidderminster.

The village had been dominated by Lord Mountnorris who began reconstructing Arley Manor as Arley Castle in the 1840s. This huge structure was demolished in 1963, but the village which nestled alongside it on the riverbank still survives, and despite some expansion remains a quiet backwater, plagued only by a few tourists brought from Bridgnorth by the railway.

The quiet village of Arley, as it appeared around 1895. The road to Arley Castle curves down to the landing stage by the river as it still does today; even though nowadays there are rather more houses, the basic tranquillity is still preserved.

A cottage alongside the road leading down to the river, with Samuel Hardwick in the gateway, and his wife Eliza behind him around 1910. This cottage was demolished in 1969 and replaced with a new house.

A view showing the essence of Arley, a rural village and harbour, in which local produce could be transported away by barge. There are carts and barrels on the bank, and boats in the water. The river was crossed by a ferry powered by the flow of the river, though nowadays a footbridge has replaced it.

Samuel Hardwick's sister and her husband, name unknown, both residents of Arley, shown around the turn of the twentieth century.

The Valentia Arms Hotel and restaurant, and beyond that the vicarage, with the tower alongside it. The tower was built by the Lord of the Manor, Lord Mountnorris, in the style of Arley Hall.

The Valentia Hotel looking the other way down to the river. At this time (1910) Arley had five other pubs, with the Crown, the Cock and the Nelson also on the east bank, and the Cider House and Harbour Inn on the other side of the river.

Arley Station in the 1920s. The Severn Valley line was open in 1862 and Arley was provided with a small station on the opposite side of the river from the main part of the village. The railway took away the river trade, but the station allowed Arley to keep its importance for shipping out local produce, and also brought in a new breed – the tourist.

The major construction on the Severn Valley Line was the Victoria Bridge over the Severn just south of Arley, taking the railway to Bewdley and then Kidderminster. To this day it remains a photogenic spot for the railway enthusiast, and this is a Collett Goods engine, No. 3205, of the Severn Valley Railway in 1984.

Arley church, dating from the twelfth century, photographed in 1969. The peel of bells on a Sunday, mixed with the sound of steam engines on the railway, and birds in the fields is an unforgettable musical symphony!

A drawing of the Harbour Inn, drawn in the 1950s. Despite its name this little pub is not alongside the river but is set on its own, half-way along the lane from the footbridge to the station.

The very tranquillity of Arley Station, set away from other buildings, makes it a natural setting for period television and film dramas, and it has starred in many. When this photograph was taken, it was in use for the TV drama *The Singing Detective*.

The opening of the Worcestershire Way, a footpath which runs along the Severn opposite Arley village. These are children from Wribbenhall First School in Bewdley. Sir Derek Barber (in the white shirt) chairman of the Countryside Commission had performed the formal opening ceremony, with a lunch in the Valentia Hotel.

The road down to the river as it appeared in 1992 at the site of Samuel Hardwick's cottage.

The village of Arley in 1992, taken from the new footbridge, which was opened in 1972.

Nine

Morville and Astley Abbotts

To the north and west of Bridgnorth are a number of attractive rural villages, such as Morville, Astley Abbotts and Stottesden. Many of them were far more important in earlier times, especially Morville, which was one of the most important towns in Shropshire during the Saxon era, but now they are just quite rural communities, lucky if their church and pub are still open, and even luckier to have a shop and a school still operating.

All these communities look to Bridgnorth for their main services, for shopping, and for its livestock market, and it is in Bridgnorth that most of the people who live in those villages come to work, now that agriculture employs so few people. Further on it is Shrewsbury and Telford which draws people.

The church of St Gregory the Great, Morville, nestling by itself in the fields, with Morville Hall behind. The present church was consecrated rather inauspiciously in 1118. On the day, when the crowd who had gathered for the consecration left for home, there was a fierce thunderstorm, and two women and five horses were killed.

The children of Morville School in 1875. Third from the left on the back row is Emma Thomas, aged seven, who only saw the sea once in her life, and everyone was surprised that she could sign her name when she got married.

The inside of Morville church around 1904, which looks exactly the same as it does today. During Saxon times Morville was one of the most important places in Shropshire.

The Acton Arms Public house in Morville as it looked before the First World War. It was named after the Acton family of Aldenham Hall, who lived just a mile away.

All the children of Morville School at their Christmas party in 1973.

A class at work in Morville School during the 1960s. Now just a two class school, the main one occupies the whole of the old hall, with the other in a new classroom outside.

The Wheatland Hunt gathered for their Boxing Day Meeting in the field between the Acton Arms and Morville church, in 1956.

St Calixtus' church, Astley Abbotts, in the 1920s. Consecrated in 1138, the church was largely rebuilt in 1633. Preserved inside is a maiden's garland and gloves, held in memory of Hannah Phillips who died on her wedding eve in 1707 while crossing the river.

The lavender field behind Astley Abbotts Hall as it appeared in 1995.

St Mary's church at Stottesden as it appeared in 1900. Stottesden was a very large Saxon parish, and part of the church dates from 1085. It still looks much the same today.

The villages of Shropshire were popular destinations for the many cycling clubs in the Black Country between the First and Second World Wars. Here the CTC from Wolverhampton is gathered outside the Boyne Arms at Burwarton on the Bridgnorth to Ludlow Road.

Ten

Worfield

The village of Worfield nestles beneath a wooded slope which shields it from the outside world, and yet Worfield parish is one of the largest in England. To motorists passing along the Bridgnorth road the public face of Worfield is actually the hamlet of Wyken, an easy mistake to make as the roadside pub is actually called the Wheel O'Worfield and the garage is called Worfield Garage. In days gone by the people who lived by the main road in Wyken would have taken umbrage at suggestions that they lived in Worfield, though they sent their children to school there and went to worship there.

Beyond the wooded slope which backs on to the church and Worfield's quaint little street, lies the rolling grounds of Davenport House and the upper part of the village, almost echoing the high and low town parts of Worfield's larger neighbour just down the road at Bridgnorth.

Clark's delivery van standing in the main street in Worfield in the 1920s. Clarks were the grocers and bakers.

Some of the notable residents of Worfield in 1887. From left to right, back row: Miss Golley (in charge of the Infants School), Mr Ormerod (church organist), Edith Lloyd (pupil teacher), Charles Tarrant (pupil teacher), Heather Thatcher (pupil teacher), Fred Lloyd (pupil teacher), Miss M.E. Evans (girls' school teacher). Front row: Mr Willoughby (curate), Mr Nicholas, Mr Lloyd (schoolmaster), Mrs Martindale (girl's school teacher).

Worfield Vicarage in 1906. This is now a hotel.

The fine avenue of trees which lead directly to the church, though only the top half of the 200ft high spire can be seen.

Church Avenue, Worfield.

Worfield church, sitting unusually at the base of a hill, and requiring all its great height to protrude above it. The bulk of the church is fourteenth century.

The building marked 'A' to the left was the old Worfield Vicarage, in use from 1617 to 1790, when it was known as the New Parsonage. The building marked 'B' to the right is the Lower Hall, a very fine half-timbered house with eighteenth century additions.

Hallon House, Worfield in 1926 when it was occupied by Walter Head and family.

Ambrose Vernon Baron and Alice Edwards on their wedding day in 1909, preparing to walk to Worfield church. Fifteen months later they had a daughter, Edith, but nine months after that Alice died, and little Edith was brought up by her aunt and uncle.

The hamlet of Wyken lies on the Bridgnorth to Wolverhampton Road, and is often mistakenly referred to as Worfield. This picture was taken around 1912.

A Wyken Lloyd family group in the 1920s, standing on the main Bridgnorth road, which has since been greatly widened. The cottage on the left was opposite the old butcher's shop, neither of which is now there. On the horse at the rear is Kath Wilcox, and among the others are Edith and Margaret Wilcox.

112

A very fine car standing outside the slaughter house on Wyken Farm in 1932, which was then farmed by John Whitefoot Wilcox.

Wyken Garage in 1937. Ten years before, it had been a blacksmith's shop which had been run by the Lloyd family since 1760, their cottage being that on the left. In 1926 it was bought and converted to a garage by George Wilcox, whose mother was a Lloyd. In the Second World War it was used for fuel storage by the US Army who were camped nearby, and it is now a butcher's shop.

A class group at Worfield school in the 1920s.

Seven girls of the country dancing team at Worfield School in the 1920s.

Boys and girls indulging in some country dancing outside Worfield School in the 1920s.

The lodge to Davenport House in the snowy winter of 1938. Davenport House was built by Francis Smith of Warwick in 1726.

The boy is John Edwards of Worfield, as a Pearly King, sitting on his steed, ready to take part in Bridgnorth Carnival in 1930. The gentleman holding the horse's head has a sign which says 'Whisper of the Derby', though the reason for this is not known.

Worfield Brownies in the 1930s.

Local women taking a dancing class in Worfield Village Hall during the Second World War.

All the children, and their mothers at Worfield School in the 1920s.

Worfield football team around 1954, posing at an away match at Tasley against AT & E of Bridgnorth. From left to right, back row: Tom Williamson, John Page, Bob Downes, Reg Fincher, ? Childs, Jim Speke. Front row: Geoff Clinton, Horace Jervis, Marcus Thomas, Allan Downes, Eddie Downes.

The Boulton Paul Aircraft Supervisors gathered for their annual dinner, inside the Wheel o' Worfield during 1962.

Eleven
Claverley and Ackleton

Claverley is a very picturesque village in which new housing developments have not greatly impinged on the central core, gathered around the Bull Ring, which is bounded by a remarkable collection of buildings. The most handsome is the half-timbered old vicarage, with the old schoolhouse alongside, both facing the King's Arms. Alongside is All Saints' church, one of the most lovely village churches in Shropshire, having been founded in Norman times, but there was undoubtedly worship on the site well before that, with indications that the church sits on the foundations of a Roman building.

Mirroring Claverley on the other side of the Bridgnorth Road, and like Claverley set near to the Dudley to Wellington Road, is the village of Ackleton. Smaller than Claverley, with only two pubs to its name, and no church or school, Ackleton is a similar quiet rural village. Both villages are now largely dormitories for Wolverhampton, pleasant retreats set just inside the beautiful county of Shropshire.

Claverly Village.

A pre-First World War view of the Bull Ring from the churchyard, with the King's Arms on the left, the fine broad lych-gate to the right, and the churchyard cross in the centre.

Further up the street is the middle one of Claverley's three Church Street pubs, the Crown, kept at the time by Emma Crowther, licensed to sell Foreign and British ales, spirits, porter, beer, cider and tobacco.

The children of Claverley School about 1910. The teacher is Mr Parry.

The Woodman Inn before 1914 with the Brazier family ranged outside. The first recorded landlord of the Woodman was Richard Brazier in 1858.

Margaret Wilcox (left) and Emma Shepherd, dressed up for Claverley Pageant in 1931. Both girls came from Worfield.

A view down Church Street in the 1930s with the Crown and then King's Head on the right, and the garage on the left. The Crown's chimney has developed a severe incline. All Saints' church was founded on 1095 by Roger de Montgomery, but the site has been used as a place of worship from Saxon times.

The Black Lion Inn at Hilton on the main Bridgnorth to Wolverhampton Road around 1930, with the car outside the gate. The Black Lion has recently closed and become a private residence.

The Edwards family children at the entrance to Young Willie Bluck's Farm at Rowley near Ackleton in 1913. On the left is Nellie (Helen Elizabeth), next to her is Walter at the rear and Harry in front. On the bike is their cousin Edith Baron, being held by George. Edith came to live with them when her mother died.

Ackleton Rovers football team in 1925. On the middle row, third from the left is Frank Clinton.

All the Ackleton village children and mothers, taking a break from a party in the village hall in celebration of the Coronation of Elizabeth II in 1953.

A drawing of the Red Cow in Ackleton, done in 1952. The extension on the side is now rather larger, as is the car park.

George Jones, landlord of the Red Cow in 1953. He had previously kept the Giffard Arms in Wolverhampton. The tiny size of the bar is in complete contrast to the large open plan room which exists today.

The Bull Ring in Claverley in the 1950s. The fine fifteenth century building in the centre is the old vicarage with the original school building to the left, now a nursery.

Claverley Women's Institute pensioners' party in the village hall in the 1950s. Included in the photograph are: -?-, Mr Francis, Mr Wilkes, Mr Morris, Mr Parker, Mr Lawley. First on the right is Mr Bowker.

Frederick George Parker, and his wife Amy, outside the Woodman in 1962. He was landlord from 1951-1976, and his father, Frederick William Parker had been landlord for ten years before that.

The Woodman's pub games presentations in 1960. From left to right, back row: Ron Hill, Ken Wright, John Wright, John Parker, -?-, Gilbert Gough. Middle row: 'Joker' Preece, Jack Barron, Frank Jones, Pauline Gough, Arthur Sneyd. Seated: John Taylor, Frederick George Parker (landlord).

Behind the bar in the King's Arms, Claverley in 1958. On the left is Ray Davies, who later emigrated to Canada, and on the right John Parker, son of the Woodman's landlord. They were giving the licencee, Arthur Palmer, a night off. Note the reel-to-reel tape recorder on the bar – is this an example of early 'muzak'?

Acknowledgements

As with all my previous books I found the people of Bridgnorth and the surrounding district very willing to lend me their photographs and share their memories. It was an absolute delight for me to investigate this beautiful area of Shropshire, and to explore places I had always meant to visit.

The starting point for this collection of photographs was the postcard collection acquired from my grandmother, Jane Brew, *née* Macham, who hailed from the Worfield area. In the days before the family owned a camera, she complied a collection of cards of the places that she knew. Many of these were used in my book *Albrighton and Shifnal*, and many more were used in this book.

I particularly have to thank the editor of the *Bridgnorth Journal*, for publishing my appeals for photographs and information, and also for letting me use some of their photographs. Other people I have to thank for lending me their photographs, or helping me in other ways are Jim Boulton, Peter Brew, Mrs V.P. Brown, Edith Bucknall, Mrs Chittleborough, Mr Geoff Clinton, Janet Corbett of Lawson Mardon Star, Mrs Laurie Davies, Patricia Dickson, Mr Foxall, Mr and Mrs Gibbons, Clive Gwilt, Mr L.S. Hall, Terry Hawkins of the Bylet Bowling Club, E.G. Jones, Morville School, Mrs M. O'Kane, Miss N. O'Kane, Mrs Patterson, John Parker, Gwen Porter, Mr Michael Royce, Mrs Shaughnessy of St Mary's School, Mrs Smallman, Allan Walford, Rosemary Wilcox, and especially Wendy Matthiason.